Glimmers
of a
Glass Heart

POEMS

C.B. Faye

Glimmers of a Glass Heart © 2025 by C.B. Faye
First Edition

ISBN: 979-8-9998521-0-6

Printed in the United States of America.

Cover design and illustrations by C.B. Faye

Published by C.B. Faye
www.cbfaye.com

You Are Not Alone

Some of the poems in this book may stir tender places.
If you're hurting, overwhelmed, or in need of someone to talk
to, please know that you never have to carry it alone.

Below are resources for safety planning and mental health
support:

988 Suicide & Crisis Lifeline
Free, 24/7, confidential support for people in distress,
prevention and crisis resources for you or your loved ones.
Call or text **988** from anywhere in the U.S.

National Domestic Violence Hotline
Support, safety planning, and resources.
Call **1-800-799-SAFE (7233)** or text **"START"** to **88788**
or chat at thehotline.org

NAMI HelpLine
For mental health guidance, education, and connection to local
resources.
Call **1-800-950-NAMI (6264)** or visit nami.org/help

For the Survivors: the ones who have been broken by the world and refuse to remain in pieces.

Contents

Part One

Collecting The Shards

The fires have ceased. Thick smoke migrates towards the sky as you crawl on hands and knees. You search in the painful dark, slicing your palms on something sharp. Fragments of your heart glimmer beneath debris. Blood warms your palms as you collect the shards. A realization hits you then – one that changes everything. Purified in the fire, your glass heart emits proof of life. Your entire world burned, and you came out alive. Your entire world burned and you –

You survived.

Fine Deception

Willing herself awake
Makeup stains her pillowcase
She prepares for the battle
Of another day
Fighting tears
Faking smiles
"I'm fine"
She persists
Keeping up appearances
For those who question
She is anything but
"Fine"

Flashbacks

Certain memories
burn my brain.
I'm trapped in time –
thoughts in flames.
Can I extinguish
the anguish
scorching my lungs?
Can I rise
from the ashes
of when I was young?

Sinking to Surface

I drown inside myself
My thoughts pull me under
My mind a silent killer
My lungs flood with fear
As I reach
To be helped
Though I know
Only I
Can save me
From myself

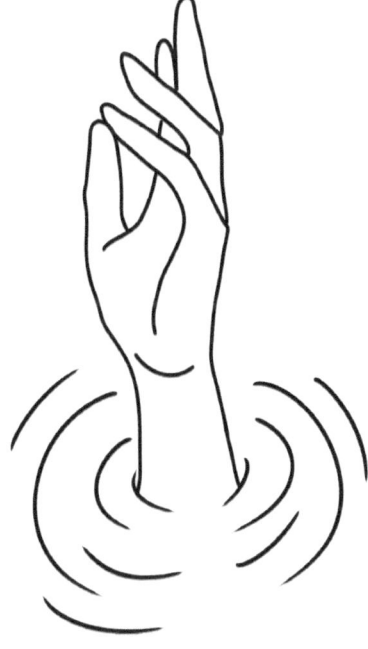

Young Faith

I cried to God
Begged for his help
No one rose from the grave
We were not saved
By heavenly grace
Or mustard seeds of faith
11 years old and *I believed*
I prayed and prayed and prayed
But no one came

Great Escape

I sit crisscross applesauce
Eyes bright with dreams
"You can grow up and be anything?!"
My books became shields
A weapon and a vice
With a brain of steel
I could finally fight
If I am smart enough
I could make it out alive

Haunted

As a child forced to survive
I buried the horrors alive
Dreams became ghosts forgotten
Night falls the hardest
On souls that are haunted

Nightmares

Pink pillows lined her bed
She built her fortress
Plush with purpose
Ordered to defend
Threatened innocence
Braced for the terrors lurking
From dusk until dawn

PTSD

Do they see what I see?
As I bravely close my eyes
Do they go where I go?
When I try to sleep at night
Do they feel the horror?
Sneaking in their bed
Do they lay to rest?
While I suffer in my head

C.B. Faye

Warzone

Home was a warzone,
Walls colored in red.
Rage filled each corner,
Ceilings hung with dread.

Home was a warzone,
Shots of trauma fired
One generation to the next.
Rounds of fear and neglect.

Home was a warzone,
Crouching behind the couch.
Hiding in the trenches,
Seeking our way out.

Home was a warzone,
Where evil won most nights.
Yet, tomorrow always came –
Another day to fight.

"Strength"

I hide the darkness
Circling my eyes
I swallow the sorrow
With phony pride
They say I am strong
When I just play the part
The strong girl
With the broken heart

Endurance

With shaky hands
and fighting eyes,
across the room,
her gaze held mine.
"Until our last breath,"
my mother sighed.

Poverty

Scarcity followed us
like an unwanted ghost
It woke us in the night
ricocheted off the walls
Mom and Dad cursed
money for it all
They told us
stories of sacrifice
riddled with guilt
We owed it to them
to bear this burden
of being alive

Inheritance

Were we born broken?
Like starving seeds
in spoiled soil
rotting at the roots.
Is it damaged DNA?
Lines of lifetimes
sewed together
by dark timelines.

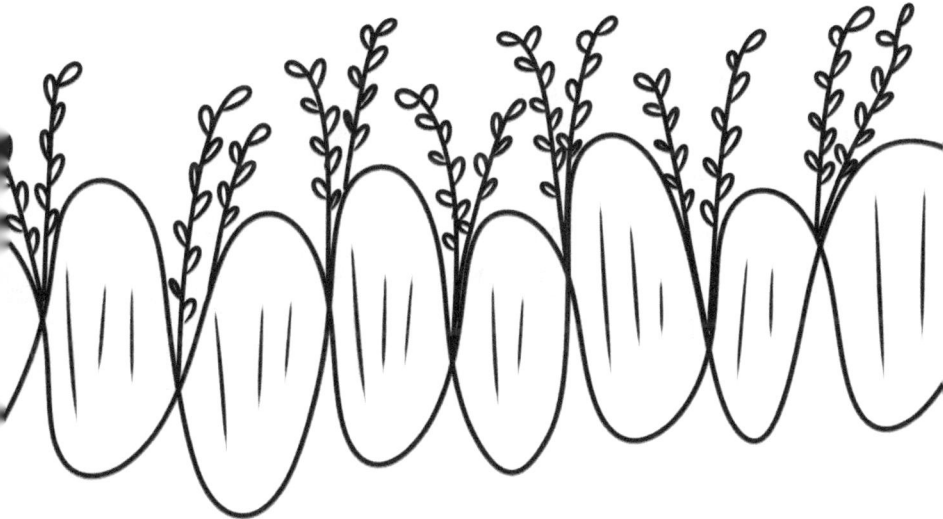

Crumbs

"What's the matter?" you ask,
And I stifle a laugh
Because I've been carving up my heart
And serving it on a platter
No matter, no matter
I'll offer myself until I'm only crumbs
Yet wonder why I feel so numb
No matter, no matter
I'll save everyone from disaster
I'm not the type to put my oxygen mask on first
Someone always has it worse
I may not be able to breathe
But maybe I'll find some relief
Knowing you won't wonder, like me,
Do I matter? Do I matter?
If that were the case,
I wouldn't let my heart race
Wouldn't try to win first place
As if self-sacrifice is a game
No matter, no matter –

I hear the irony in my words
The heartbreak in this verse
Like caring could be a curse
But there *is* a portrait of me
Describing compassion fatigue
Then I act like my apathy
Is this grand mystery
When...
I've been carving up my heart
And serving it on a platter
Pretending like...
Like I don't matter

Odds

Can you win
in a world
betting against you?

Breathless

Some pain cuts so deep
it breaks skin,
filling every pore.
It lives in your gut,
retrieving dinner
from your bowels.
Some pain
lodges in your throat,
choking your cries.
It kicks your ribs in,
knocking the breath
right out of you.

Alive

I must remind myself sometimes:
I'm 25 and I'm alive.
Have you ever been scared for your life?
My first time I was 5.
I'd close my eyes and disappear.
Anywhere but here.
I spent most of my life thinking I would die.
So, I remind myself sometimes:
I'm 25 and I'm alive.
I open my eyes and reappear.
Right now, I am here.

Conscience

I still wonder
How you sleep at night
If your conscience turns to stone
When you close your eyes

Just Breathe!

They make it sound so easy
Like I *choose* this anxiety
But my shallow lungs
and racing heart
refuse to forget...
We were not safe
We had to escape
My body and brain
chose to part ways
Now I search for my breath
in the parts of me that left
"Just breathe!"
It's just... not that easy

Marathon

My heart bends over
hands on her knees
gasping for air
trying to breathe
"Slow down!"
She begs my mind
each thought
a hurdle I climb

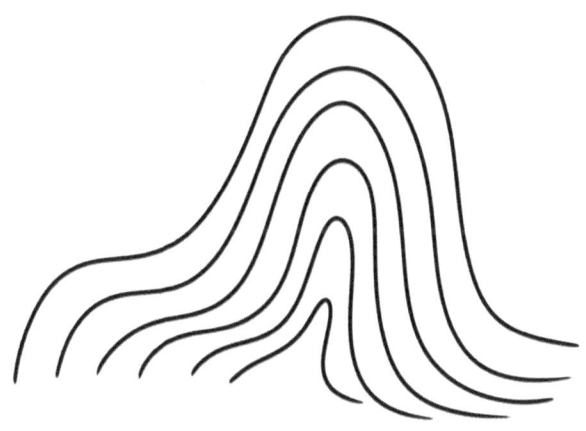

Dreamer's Curse

Some days
my potential
sets a fire
to my soul
Other days
my distant dreams
leave me dying
to be whole

Validation

Working for worth
Is a way of life
For the broken
For those who earned love
Given upon approval
Collecting praises like gold stars
Forever hoping they were enough

Lonely Lust

Fleeing from cover to cover
One lover to another
Soul-seeking in between fleece
Searching for love on your knees
Body after body
Crying yourself to sleep
Waking up wishing
It was love that stained your sheets

C.B. Faye

Endless Search

I search everywhere
Underneath men
Approval in friends
My own reflection
I search and search and search
For my worth
In my father's lies
In my mother's eyes
The soul's demise
To search and search and search
For your worth

Thoughts That Aren't Mine

Even when life is kind
Evil echoes in my mind
Thoughts that aren't mine:
It's too good to be true!
Honey, they don't like you.
You don't deserve happiness,
Don't you feel this emptiness?
Life has been unkind
So even when I hear these lies
Evil echoes in my mind
Thoughts that aren't mine

Fragments

How do you become whole
when parts of your soul
lay spread across time?
Will I spend my life
collecting the fragments
of pieces parted by pain?

Walking Blind

Is it the world
that's against me
or is it my mind?
Surely my life
confirms my doubt
as problems arise,
impassable heights
no one could climb.
Progress looms
beyond the bounds
of possibility.
Don't you see what I see
or am I walking blind?
Is it the world
that's against me
or is it my mind?

Depression

Losing the will
to eat
to laugh
to exist
is not pretty
There is nothing romantic about depression
it takes
and takes
and takes
until you believe
life was always this way –
e m p t y

Prisoner

I am the ball
and the chain
I am the lion
and the cage
I am the tamer
and the tamed
Almost free
still enslaved

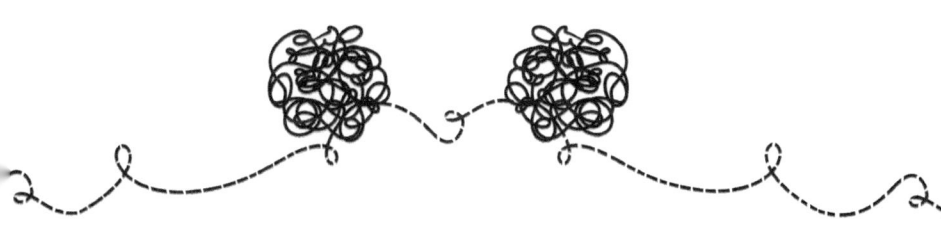

C.B. Faye

Aimless

Anxiety is like a rocking chair
It brings you back and forth
But gets you nowhere

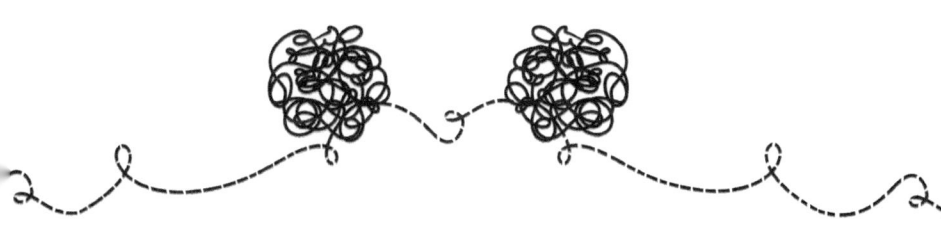

Wasteland

I let the flowers die
Broken, brown, and brittle
I saw myself in their plight
Thirsty, hungry, little
I panicked at the sight
When did self-care
Become impossible
Why is wellness
Another obstacle
How could I
Waste my privilege
How could I
Could I
I
Let the flowers die

C.B. Faye

Surrender

I lay down in the silence
"I can't bear this weight,"
I admit to the moonlit night.
"It is not yours to bear alone,"
The winking stars replied.
I unclenched my fists
Turned my palms towards the sky,
"You may take what is not mine."
The wind rustled in response
Drifting away the sharp edges
Piercing my bleeding heart

EXISTENCE

There are days
the Earth could
open its sultry core
and swallow me whole
Other days
life is a maze
trapped in a fog
lost at each turn
Yet some days...
hope sneaks in
laughing with friends
the sun on my skin
Living is feeling all of it

When Panic Attacks

Threats unseen ambush me
Panic sounds the alarms
Each nerve signals danger
How do I respond?
My thoughts scream, "RUN!"
But my legs lost their will
I could stay and fight
But I'll die on that hill
Blood races to my heart
Recalling what I left
I locate that power
And inhale a deep breath

Letting Go

To the river I went
a soul full of bricks
I envied the water
gliding so gently
Over rock and stone
moving so freely
it flows
      and flows
           and flows

Sleeping Giants

Doubt cowers
Before my destiny
Spewing lies
Designed to distract
The power inside
If I don't believe in me
Fear takes the lead
So thoughts tiptoe
Near my dreams
Afraid to awake
My greatness

Symphony

The curtains swish open
And fear takes center stage
Pain hums the melody
Shame and doubt duet
Insecurity, a quartet
The anxious ensemble
Insists I join their act
But I prefer the audience
Where I am just a witness

Jailbreak

Passion burns inside me
Flames with no trail to blaze
My diseased disposition
Is a soul which is caged
My heart knows salvation
Is in and of itself
When I release my fear
I will free myself

Whispers of the Weeping Willow

Slouched against a willow tree
Ancient wisdom speaks to me,
"I sway with my sorrow
And let my branches weep.
Sadness lives on my leaves,
A mere extension of me.
You are not spoiled soil
Or the thirsty seed beneath.
You are the whole tree –
The strongest roots run deep."

Hearts Like Mine

Worrying doesn't change anything. I have scoured for evidence
to prove my worries made a difference. There is none. I relay
these findings to my anxious heart. But I don't just wear my
heart on my sleeve. It lives beyond my body. It bleeds in the
open, for everyone to see. This is my triumph and my
downfall. Hearts like mine do not just care... we *really* care...
we worry. Excessively. We feel it all – for everyone and
everything – at risk of drowning in our own depths. Hearts
like mine burn for the people we love. But burning ourselves
alive saves no one. We must shield our hearts from the worries
we weaponize. A heart on fire can torch the mind.

EMOTION

We enter this world
sobbing out the womb
All of us begin life
with oceans in our eyes
Somehow, we forget
we were *born to cry*
We spend our lives
shaming emotion
Denying the *very thing*
that makes us human

Pursuit of Happiness

How come
our own arms
our own spirits
our own hearts
are always
the last resort?
We go looking
for answers
inside things
inside bottles
inside bodies
anywhere but,
inside ourselves.
We were taught
all we want
and all we need
exists outside ourselves
and still we wonder:
Why am I unhappy?

To Love a Survivor

If you love someone wounded by the world:
You must see them, dive into their dark.
See them as whole, not the sum of their parts.

If you can see them and love them as they are –
Prepare to discover beauty buried beneath.
You'll find a heart still beating as it bleeds.

Pure and precious and rarer than gold –
You'll find a heart forged in the fire.
This will be your gift: *to love a Survivor*

Mental Illness

What does healing look like
In societies who forgo
Empathy for profiting?
What does healing look like
For the sick who can't admit
The monsters in their minds?
How do you heal
When your medicine is mocked?
How do you heal
When you're expected to move on?
How do you heal
Like nothing's wrong?
Like your mind isn't a ticking time bomb?
Like 1 in 5 won't lose their lives
To a disease we only speak of
When we close the blinds.

Empathy

Fear breeds violence
Darkness brews in silence
Our hearts walk in disguise
Blind to our own demise
Pain is the proof we all bleed
Love is the cure we all need
To be human is to suffer
To rise we lift each other

Cosmic Crossroads

Humanity stands
At a cosmic crossroads:
Fear   or   Love
This is the choice –
Extinction   or   Evolution
We decide our fate.

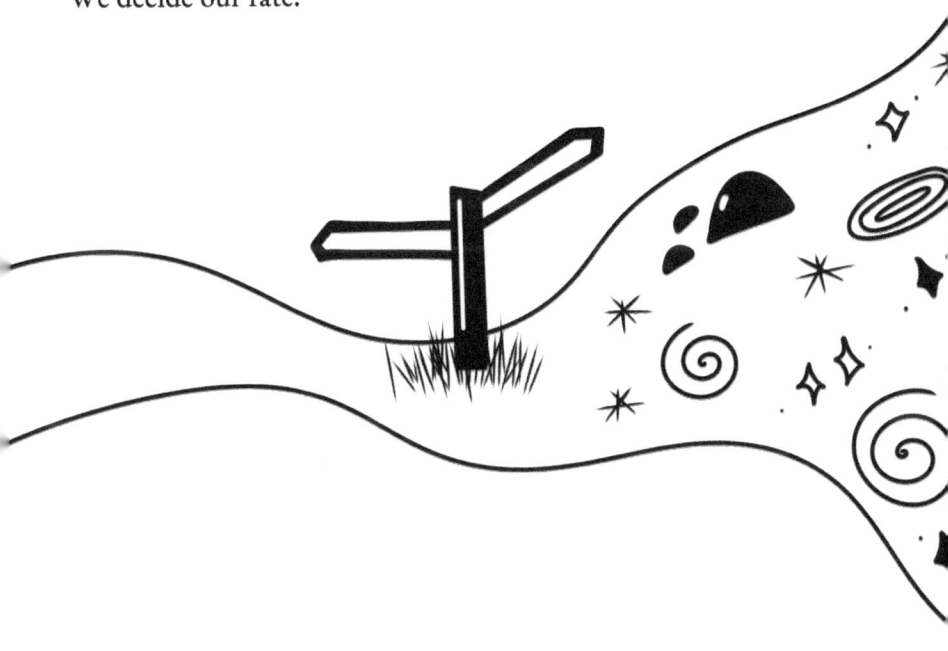

Rock Bottom

Buried beneath my demons
I tasted the bitter earth
I rose from the ground
With a mouthful of dirt
I used to fear rock bottom
But I've been here before
Now the devil starts running
When I show up at his door

Old Friend

I toast my demons on the weekends!
I lay naked with sorrow
and bathe in my shadows.
I get coffee with my shame
and picnic with my pain.
Darkness is an old friend,
we are mates for life.
I must keep him close,
where he can see the light.

Unfortunate

I must bet on myself
If angry gods dealt my cards
I cannot fold
Or curse my odds
If life is a game
I play for keeps
My hopeless hand
Will not define me

Survivor

I was born fighting
Where the sun couldn't reach
I rose through the cracks
Wherever you plant me
A flower in concrete
I will *always* bloom

Multidimensional

We see ourselves as static
characters on a single page
we abandon the past
when we are every age –
every age we've ever been
the teenager with angst
once a child with dreams
forgotten as adults
each part of us still needs –
needs to be seen   and heard   and loved

Carry your shadows to the light
they are the pieces pain left behind.

Investments

I thought maturing meant
Shunning my shredded soul
But pain demands a price
I had to pay the toll
It costs more to avoid
Than it does to feel it all

Healing

I'm taking each piece life broke
Collecting the shards
Smoothing the edges
Mending my glass heart
As a mosaic of broken parts

Part Two

Mending Our Hearts

Do not let the darkness convince you that a broken heart will never become whole. Yes, you are in pieces. Pain has shattered your glass heart. There will be certain parts of your heart that you may never recover. Trauma is a thief. But for all its efforts, trauma doesn't take everything. Somehow, someway, fragments of your soul remain. Your heart may never be the same because our hearts are built to break. *This* is the power of a glass heart —

It refuses to remain in pieces.

Homesick

My weary soul
Lays down to rest
From dusk to dawn
She walked the line
She lost herself
A thousand times
Tonight, she sleeps
In her bed alone
For now, she found
Her glass heart is home

Groundbreaking

If the light was lost on me
I'd become the sun herself
Turn my wounds into water
Let the pain make me stronger
Grow gardens from promises
Of roots sewn in darkness
If the light was lost on me
I'd challenge the sun herself
In a race to the horizon
Imagine her surprise when
My pain fulfilled its purpose
And I broke through the surface

Trailblazer

On the coldest nights
Her rage kept her warm
Vengeance for lost innocence
Kept her moving forward
In her arms she carried
The children she had been
"Never again," she promised
To end ages of violence

Trauma

Trauma changes everything
One is never the same
After grieving all
That trauma took
Innocence, safety, self-esteem
Trauma is a thief!
Therefore, I grieve:
For the childhood
I will never see
For the father
Mine could not be
Trauma changes everything
For when your heart breaks
It cracks wide open
A broken heart makes space
To let more love in
One is never the same
After healing all
It cost to survive
Anger, despair, and self-blame
Healing changes everything

The Truth Scars Tell

To the ones who are lost,
inside the world
inside themselves:
You may not believe
a better tomorrow is in reach.
You may not see
the light in the cracks underneath.
You may not know
a life outside your shadow.
I hear your silent cry,
you wish to escape this life.
But child there is peace
in the air that you breathe.
The scars that paint you
is the art which made you.
The answers that you seek
are closer than you think.
Visit your darkness,
take in its fullness.
Talk to your demons
heed their teachings.

How Do We Let The Light In?

We sift through our pain
Traverse the muddy waters
We cleanse what was
And accept what is

How do we let the light in?

We

Filter

Out

The

Dark

Freedom

Surf the shadows
Embrace the unseen
Visit the wounds
Bleeding beneath
Your freedom is waiting
In whatever you're facing
Pain is not a prison
It is your liberation

Perspective

The world you see
is not lost on me.
The good isn't gone
no, only forgotten.
You may have lost
a line of sight,
but soon you'll wake
to a deeper truth.
The light will *never*
be lost on you.

Broken People

You are not weak for being broken.

Weakness is outrunning the truth
Strength means facing your wounds.
Cowardice is hiding in the dark
Warriors live with a bleeding heart.

You are not weak for being broken.

No, you are not weak for *being human.*

Love Remains

The Loss –
A twisted knife
An angry thorn
A heart torn
From the Love
We have Lost
The Injustice of
Them being gone
Seeking, pleading, screaming
In the ruins of Grief...
Gleaming in the dark
Something lights a spark
Memories come to life
Laughter fills the night
Somehow, someway...
Joy seeps in
Through shattered glass
Each moment you had
Reflects within
Your broken heart
Buried beneath the
Mountains of Pain
Somehow, someway...
Love remains

Twilight Portraits

Maybe this sunset
Is unlike any other
Maybe they are up there
Your lover, brother, mother
Painting the sky
With your favorite colors
Maybe they know
On this ordinary night
You are looking up
Searching for a sign
So, they paint the sky
A tapestry of hues
Twilight portraits
Made just for you

C.B. Faye

You are the Warrior

You are not
the pain
or the heartbreak.
You are not
the darkness
or the wound.
You are
the heart
and the skin.
You are
the light
and the soul
fighting against it all.

Ever-flame

A spark of connection catches you off-guard. You feel a small moment of joy. A lightness surprises you. Glimmering in the dark, your spirit is an ever-flame. However fleeting, you felt it. At long last, you felt *something*.

Being Human

No one escapes being human,
But oh, how we try!
To run from ourselves
And dodge the demons.
We consume anything
To avoid our feelings.
Still, we're surprised
When the pain remains.
As if human suffering
Heals with band-aids.
Yes,
It hurts like *Hell* to be human.
The only way out is going through it!

Peace

A state of being we yearn to gain
You feel it in falling rain
You sense it in ocean waves
A treasure buried in our pain

Phoenix

A moment will come.
When the life you've lived is no longer the life you lead.
The anguish will pass through you like a subtle breeze.
Gravity will bear its weight on you as it does for everyone else.
But this time, your knees will not buckle. Your legs may
tremble but this time – you will rise.
A moment will come.
When you stare down the face of darkness and stay to meet its
maker. You will declare it met its match. You will dive into the
depths of your soul and finally remember how to swim.
You will slay the belly of the beast. You will starve the demons
once and for all.
A moment will come.
When you greet your brokenness and discover the light in the
cracks. You will travel to your edges and caress its beauty for
the first time. You will remove the thorns from your flesh.
You will inhale a breath from long ago. A new dawn will break
the horizon. From the ashes you will take form.
The moment will *come.*
When you are born anew.

You Are Here

Heels in
Head up
Fists clenched
Raise them up
Look around
Stand tall
You are here
Through it all

Reflection

Come child.
Sit down
at the table
with yourself.
Stare into
the eyes
of whom
needs you most.
Reach for
your hand
and don't let go.

Uncharted

Your soul is water
Stray from the shore
Dive into the depths
Surf the unknown
Discover what is lost
Come back home

Hero

You are here to serve
As the hero of your own life
This duty calls for no one else
You are here to save yourself

Wayfinder

Healing your soul
has no one path
The journey within
without a map
The deeper you go
the darker it gets
Monsters in the shadows
demons in the night
Fear chains your feet
              with
        no
     end
    in
sight
Defeated in the dark
knees meet the ground
At the floor of your pain
salvation is found
A light faintly flickers
a light you once lost
Ba-dum, ba-dum, ba-dum
shines the beat of your heart

Burned, bruised, and broken
you rise in the night
No need to know the way
                because
            you
        found
    the
light

Sailing

The sadness fades
The fear weakens
The worry drifts
And the pain heals
Stay afloat
The storm calms
The winds settle
The sun returns
And the seas will still
Stay afloat

Self-evident

Every breath you take is proof
That you are exactly
(Inhale)
Where you are meant to be
(Exhale)
Every day you wake is evidence
That you are worthy
(Inhale)
For simply being alive
(Exhale)

Rotten Roses

Sometimes healing asks us to smell the rotten roses. To consider the patterns and people whose sweet aroma soured. The old beliefs which never flowered. Sometimes the familiar is the cost of growth. So, there is a loneliness in letting go. Seasons of solitude yet to yield peace. You can hold onto this bouquet of decay, or you can empty the vase. Wash the dirty water down the drain. Replace what you knew with what could be. Plant a self-sufficient seed. Sometimes healing asks us to smell the rotten roses.

Towards the Light

There is an order to it all
How we wilt and we rise
Seeds planted in darkness
Always grow towards the light

Autumn's Promise

September's vengeful sun
Bleached all color from June
Grief clung to skin, a heavy haze
A Summer dream gone too soon
Autumn arrived with caution
Bearing a tender promise
Her rusty yellow leaves
Curling in the cool breeze
Her proof of solidarity
Lay fallen at our feet
Autumn bids us remember
No season lasts forever

Better Days

May you learn to love the rain
As days dressed in gray
Remind us
When the skies return blue
Better days were on the way

Listen

Earth strums a melody
Bees hum the chorus
Life sings in harmony
Birds chirp in tune
Your soul is a symphony
Cells made of music
Dancing DNA
Your heart beats for you

C.B. Faye

Growth is a Process

Like the monarch
with fresh wings
flying takes time.
Oh yes, my dear
even you –
especially you.
Oh, how you will fly!

Rebirth

Becoming
all
that
you
are
is
Shedding
all
that
you
are
not

C.B. Faye

The Other Side

She stands in disbelief.
Off in the distance,
Hope glistens in the sky.
She hears a song,
A truth from long ago.
The wind whispers,
"Your time has come."
She peers behind her
As mountains she climbed
Shrink out of sight.
She stands in disbelief –
For she has arrived.

Appraisal

I've been taught
To hate my muchness
My edges
And my roughness
I am not
Up for discussion
Women are not
Problems to be solved
Your calculation
For our perfection
Is a failing formula
You could never measure
The worth of a woman

Divine Dynasty

Pedestals of patriarchs
Cowards crowned in vain
Wars waged in ego
Thrones made of rage
Blinded by aggression
Their rule nears its end
She rises from the fire
Blazing as the sun
The Queen resurrected
For her kingdom: she comes

Undone

Girl, take it off
Remove your jeans
Disrobe the day
Unhook your bra
Exhale the pain
Layer by layer
Give yourself permission
To come undone

Protest

I refuse to be
The quiet girl
Brooding in the corner
Sitting on her opinions
I refuse to reduce
My space in a room
Catering to your comfort
Preserving your fragility
I refuse to assume
The role scripted
For every woman
To be seen and not heard
I refuse

Potential

Tear the roof off
your self-doubt
You are known
across the galaxy
The skies gossip
of your power
Earth spins
in your favor
Your voice commands
the ocean tides
Each step you take
echoes in time
You inspire
all of creation
See yourself
among the stars
Free yourself
To shine as you are

More Than Enough

You are:
Seen
Forgiven
Worthy
Capable
Beautiful
Whole
And Loved
Just as you are:
More than enough

The World Needs You

Something lives within you
That the world needs
Gifts unwrapped
Talents undiscovered
Unique offerings
Worthwhile creations
Not yet expressed
No one can say it
Like you
No one can dream it
Like you
No one can think it
Like you
There is (*literally*) no one
Like you
Something lives within you
That the world needs

Like Water

Life is a cosmic dance that you cannot always lead. You must surrender to how and where the world moves you. You need to have faith in your partner. Take the universe with your shaky hands and let it guide you in each measure. Move with life like water. Let yourself take the form of each moment you're in. Slide into uncertainty. You will not arrive alone. *Dance.*

Alone?

You share each morning
with the sun.
The birds wake you
with their hum.

The trees embrace you
in each breeze,
they walk with you,
each fallen leaf.

The clouds carry you
through each day,
looking over you,
so you're okay.

The moon tucks you in
each passing night.
She pulls you close
and hugs you tight.

As a child of
the world itself,
you're never alone,
or by yourself.

What If?

What if you're closer than you've ever been before? What if
you're closer to loving yourself and loving your life than you've
ever been? What if your fears are becoming afraid of you?
What if your dreams are reaching for you too? What if any
change you've attempted to make, no matter how small, have
tipped the scales completely?

One Day (Soon)

One day
You will wake
Differently than before
You will breathe
New life in your lungs
You will see a light
Once forgotten
One day
The better tomorrow
Will be today

C.B. Faye

You Are Everything

The Universe rolled up its sleeves / dripped in elbow grease /
when it created you / gathered the sun's rays and painted your
eyes / copied songbirds to craft your voice / plucked stars from
midnight skies / sprinkling each freckle on your face / you
simply cannot be insignificant / when you are matter itself / a
million miracles / you are everything the light touches / all the
shadows in between / more than enough / you are *everything*.

Unity

I see you
Every part of your soul
Each broken bit
The places you don't feel whole

I hear you
The wounds that remain
All the shadows that linger
The scars you bear today

I love you
Each shattered piece
Every fragment lost
All the darkness beneath

You are worthy
Every part of your soul
Each broken bit
The places you don't feel whole

Homebody

Your body is your home,
the planet of your soul.
Whatever shape it takes,
or curves that form,
however vast or slim –
a sturdy shelter
for every miracle
within.

Living Love

Let love flow
like blood runs
in your veins
Breathe in love
as the air
fills your lungs
Is it not your heart which keeps you alive?
We are living love
Return to love
Like the rain
joins the sea
Love is your nature
set yourself free

Gentle Hearts

Her heart was a rebellion
Legends say when she loved
The sun danced out of the clouds
Flowers bloomed in the night
The hard world grew soft
For the gentle to survive

Loving is an Art

I want my energy to be felt in a room. Not in an embracive way. I strive to be grounded in the soil of my soul. To recalibrate the energy of anything and anyone I encounter. I want to be the crisp mountain air people only inhale on occasion. I want to be the sight of a yellow horizon and embody all the promises a new day brings. I wish to be everything the light touches and everything it doesn't. That's where love is needed most. Being Love is being all of it. The heart which breaks and the heart which builds. Loving is an art. I wish to be every color.

Love in a Sea of Stars

Rivers can't love oceans
like stars refuse the moon
As rivers envy
the sea's abundance and
stars mock
the moon's radiance But
the deep blue knows like
the starless sky where a
river flows
and what lights the night
Your heart may sink
in the depths of mine
but love is a current you
can swim if you try

Sea Glass

Most tread lightly through my soul. They scan my shores and measure my depths before retreating to the shallows. Every so often someone will come along and get their feet wet. Swimming at their own risk, careful not to fall in. My soul is sea glass, forged by shrieking winds and hungry waves. I am no stranger to these seas. I sail my soul with ease. If it is smooth waters you need, you are no sailor to me.

Mundane Magic

The moon sets
While your breath
Whispers me awake
In folds of blue cotton
I sink in your embrace
The eager sun joins us
Sooner than we wish
We grumble and stir
But happiness is this
Sharing the ordinary
The moments in between
Love is the reality
That makes life a dream

Half-light

If the sun lost the moon
She would still rise
The world would still spin
But only half as bright
To live without you
An ocean without tides
I would spend each night
Looking for your light

C.B. Faye

Lighthouse

Sailing through the dark
Your light led the way
You found my panicked soul
And signaled her with grace
Drowning in the depths
Your heart rescued mine
You saved a sinking spirit
And brought her back to life

As Love Matures

As love matures
It loses a need for words
Though I'll still try to
Write the perfect verse
A foolish attempt
To describe a love
Which leaves me speechless...
As love matures
It resembles a hearth
A fire that slowly burns
Sparks in the mundane
Emit a steady warmth
For the rest of our days
I vow to kindle the flame

Shameless

Shouldn't love be corny? A boasting, grandiose display of affection and admiration. Love lives free of shame. Love is not embarrassed. This is its power. Where our minds may hesitate; Love takes the leap. Love just knows. It speaks in whispers for those willing to listen. To love is to surrender. A courageous act of allowing the heart to open and trusting where it leads. An open heart has likely been broken. So, when Love rewards those brave enough to love again, let them rejoice. Let Love be cringey and corny and cute. Remember, Love lives free of shame. It is a force which prevails either way.

Too Good to be True

I spent my entire life imagining you
Dreaming about your smile
How my name would sound
Falling from your parted lips
The kind of father you would be
One, I hoped, who was
Different than mine
You would be gentle
And truly kind
If I was brave enough
To reveal my shadows
You would stay to face them
You would clear the clouds
Blocking my heart's light
You would be the one –
My eternal sun
I spent my entire life imagining you
Forgive me if you still seem
Too good to be true

Utopia

To wake up in a world
That's fallen in love with itself
What would that world look like?
If each person
Took the brave journey
Of embracing who they are
To heal their wounds
To conquer themselves
Rather than justifying
Our existence
In division
In war
In violence
A world that's fallen in love with itself
Wouldn't be a perfect world
But it would be a world that's trying
Moving towards compassion
Growing beyond hate
Reaching for acceptance
A world that's fallen in love with itself
Wouldn't fear our differences
But rejoice in the beauty
Of each unique soul

Mystery

Maybe the point is
To leave life a mystery
We're hell-bent on seeking
Desperate to make meaning
Tell me the point
Of knowing how and why
When the true miracle
Is simply being alive
To fill your nails with dirt
To gaze upon the sky
To fall head over heels
In love with your life
Maybe the meaning
Is in the mystery

C.B. Faye

Forevermore

All hearts begin as glass
Destined to break in half
We arrive feeling everything
We love, we hope, we dream
We lose, we hurt, we grieve
No one is shatterproof
Some people place up walls
Some choose to feel nothing at all
Those who pick up the pieces
Wield power with their pain
A heart which transforms
Is a heart which lasts
Forevermore

127

Foresight

I wonder how she knew
How she knew even then
About the beauty of life
And where to find the light
How she knew even when
Her prayers went unheard
Her faith was undeterred
I wonder if she knew
That *it does gets better*
Because I showed her the proof –
Visions from the future
Warm rooms and love given freely
Promises of peace and safety
Perhaps the hope she held onto
Was not naiveté, but foresight
Perhaps she always knew
That *there is more to life*
Because the woman I am today
Showed her we would survive
Because the woman I am today
Vowed that we would thrive
For the hope she held onto
Was not naiveté, but foresight

Healing is time-traveling through the soul.

**Our charge is to collect the shards and mend our hearts
with the broken parts.**

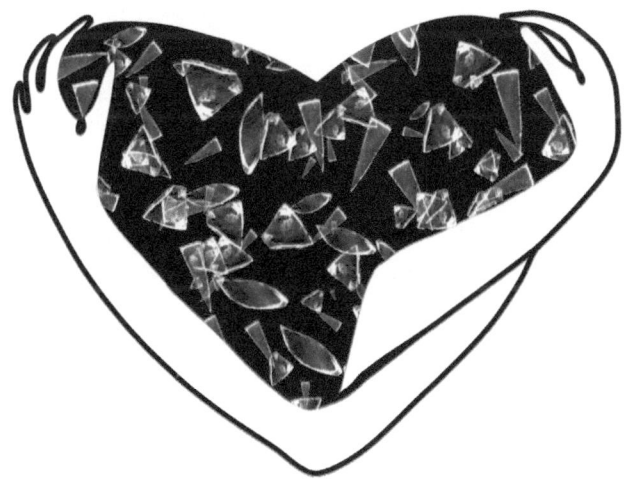

Acknowledgements

To my endlessly supportive husband, Nick: thank you for believing in me and championing every dream of mine! Your support never wavers, your love mends and polishes my glass heart, your spirit lightens every dark room I find myself in. You are my biggest dream come true – always.

To my parents, for every sacrifice amidst impossible odds, thank you. I hope the triumph and healing I found in these words can reflect the struggles you have overcome and the victories you have won.

To my siblings, the best thing about childhood was growing up with you. To Kayla, Jarred, and Isaiah, thank you for celebrating every milestone in life! To Todd, your feedback and artistic insight has been invaluable, thank you for being YOU.

To my found family, the women who helped me believe I was a *real* writer – Christina, Emily, Summer, Claire, Giuliana, and Kendall – thank you for championing my words from the beginning, for honoring every truth I was scared to tell. To Adele, Hannah, and Lauren, who always cheer me on and reassured me these words should be in the world. To my girl gang (GG!) – you are my muses, thank you for supporting my writing journey for all these years.

Finally, the beautiful people I had the courage to write this book for: you, my dear reader. Thank you for allowing my words into your heart. My greatest hope is that you found pieces of yourself in these stories. That your Glass Heart felt seen between these pages. I am eternally grateful for you.

About the Author

For as long as she can remember, C.B. Faye has turned to words as a place of refuge and release. Based in Charlotte, North Carolina, she writes with raw honesty and vivid imagery, weaving together stories of heartbreak, healing, resilience, and self-love. Her work reflects the deep currents of mental health, trauma recovery, and feminism, inviting readers to find pieces of themselves within her pages. Beyond writing, Faye is a practicing mental health professional, avid fantasy reader, and indulges in any time outdoors with her animals and husband.

Stay Close

If you felt held between these pages, our story doesn't end here!

I'm slowly building a growing circle of Glass Hearts – for those who feel deeply and crave authenticity. Who believe in healing, humanity, and hope. For more poetry and spoken word:

Join us on Instagram and TikTok @c.b.faye

www.cbfaye.com

From my Glass Heart to yours — thank you for reading. Let's keep finding the glimmers, the beauty in our brokenness, the resilience of a heart which beats despite it all.

Index

Index

Index

Index

Index

www.ingramcontent.com/pod-product-compliance
Lightning Source LLC
Chambersburg PA
CBHW021205130626
46554CB00005B/2002